24

With special thanks to the entire Compendium family.

CREDITS

Written by: Jennifer Pletsch

Designed by: Jill Labieniec

Edited by: Robin Lofstrom

Creative direction by: Sarah Forster

ISBN: 978-1-935414-72-8

1st Printing. Printed in China with soy inks.

YOU MAKE THE WORLD BETTER

Written by Jennifer Pletsch
Designed by Jill Labieniec

COMPENDIUM®
INCORPORATED

Those who bring

SUNS

to the lives of othe

HINE

annot keep it from themselves.

j. m. barrie

YOU ARE A LIGHT

...we make a life by what we

GIVE.

winston churchill

YOU ADD JOY
TO EVERY DAY

Go out into the world and do goo

til there is too much good in the

RLD.

larry h. miller

YOU MAKE LIFE
SWEETER

Blessed are those who can gi

REMEM

thout

BERING

and take without forgetting.

elizabeth bibesco

YOU ARE AN
NSPIRATION

By being yourself, you put something

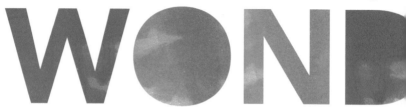

ERFUL

in the world that was not there before.

edwin elliot

YOU ADD EXTRA TO THE
ORDINARY

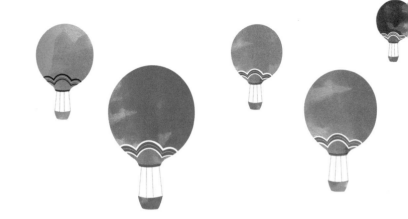

A kind

WORD

is like a spring day

russian proverb

YOU MAKE EACH DAY MORE
BEAUTIFUL

our thoughts, words and deeds are

PAINTING

the world around you.

jewel diamond taylor

YOU ARE
A MARVEL

pread love

WHEREVER

you go...

mother teresa

YOU ADD HEART
TO ALL YOU DO

What a difference one

PERSON

can make

sasha azeve

YOU ARE ONE-OF-A-KIND
WONDERFUL

Act your

HEART.

There's nothing else.

theodore roethke

May

HAPP

touch your life today as warmly a

INESS

ou have touched the lives of others.

rebecca forsythe